The Prestige S

Middlesbrough and Stockton

Philip Battersby

© **2002 Venture Publications Ltd**
ISBN 1 898432 30 9

Cover: The rich blue and cream colours of Middlesbrough Corporation enhance the neat lines of the Northern Counties bodies on Daimler Fleetline No. **126** (**RDC 126**) and lowbridge Guy Arab No.**18** (**JDC 218**). The attention to detail which produces a livery of this quality is to be found in the black and gold lining and gold fleet numbers, the absence of external advertising and the five coats-of-arms on each bus. Building works have since changed this 1963 scene opposite the Town Hall beyond recognition. *(Author's Collection)*

Rear cover: The green livery of Stockton Corporation *(top)* was quite a deep shade, but often described as "light" by people who were unquestioningly comparing it with the dark green used by the Tees-side Railless Traction Board *(bottom)*. The Stockton depot yard view in 1966 shows Nos **59** and **60** (**KPT 764/5**) and another of the few remaining 1949 Massey-bodied Leyland PD2/3s, whilst the pair of TRTB trolleybuses passing their depot in 1963 are 1944 Sunbeams Nos **16** and **17** (**CPY 287/8**) which had been rebodied in 1961 and 1962 respectively. *(Author's Collection)*

Title page: These bus stops at Middlesbrough Road East, South Bank, served a populous township and a busy shopping area. One afternoon in 1967 passengers were boarding Sunbeam trolleybus No. **1** (**GAJ 11**) of the Tees-side Railless Traction Board for the short trip home to Grangetown, overlooked by the ever-present blast furnaces. The Board's T motor bus service and the ubiquitous United buses each had their own stops separate from those of the trolleybuses. *(Author)*

Opposite page: Stockton's High Street and parish church is the setting for this fine portrait of No. **99** (**VUP 464**), one of the Corporation's three Crossley-bodied Leyland PD2/12 models of 1957. This batch of 63-seaters achieved a new maximum seating capacity for the Tees-side municipal operators at the time, but were joined almost at once on the same streets by some Northern vehicles with Park Royal bodies, almost identical even to the VUP registrations. *(Photobus)*

Below: A quiet moment in Middlesbrough Corporation's depot yard in 1962 revealed a goodly selection of the 1949 Leyland PD1/3 models with bodies by Eastern Coach Works. Numbers **67**, **58**, **64** and **68** with matching registrations from the **ADC 653-68** sequence were facing the camera whilst Guy Arabs Nos **34** and **36** (**BXG 134**, **DXG 136**) faced the wall. *(Ron Maybray)*

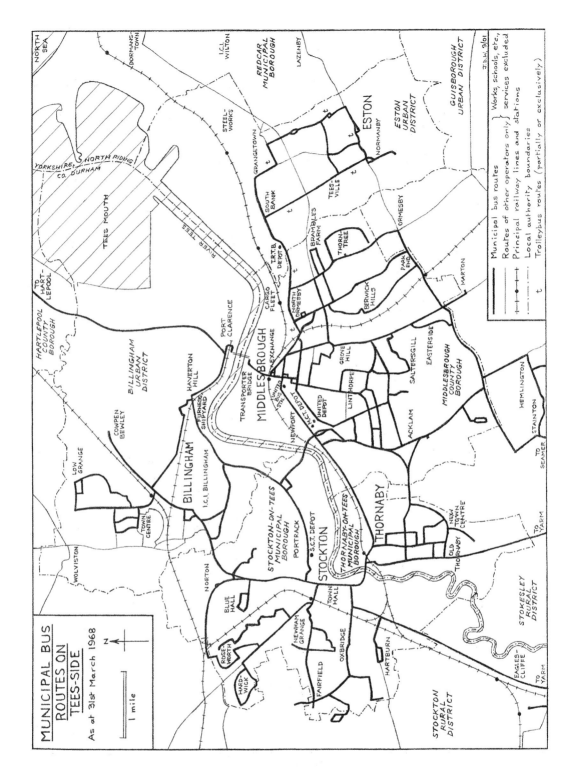

This map has been specially drawn for this book by John D. Watson. No previous maps have shown the pre-1968 municipal undertakings at their final stage of development, either separately or together. The subsequent maps of Teesside Municipal Transport show significant changes to routes and services. Apart from depicting the extent of the trolleybus system, it has unfortunately not been possible in the available space to give details of individual operators and services.

4

INTRODUCTION

This is a book about the municipal buses of Middlesbrough, Stockton-on-Tees and district, a densely populated industrial area in the north-east of England. Those buses are no longer in municipal ownership, so our subject matter is inevitably in the past, but that is where we want it to be; there are other books for those whose interests are more contemporary. Many other buses, operated by large companies and by independents, have served this area over the years, but this volume is about the activities of the Middlesbrough and Stockton corporation undertakings and the Tees-side Railless Traction Board, with some reference to the immediate successors of all three. These successors were Teesside Municipal Transport in 1968 and Cleveland Transit in 1974. A fourth municipal operator for most of our period was West Hartlepool Corporation, which is featured briefly.

Stockton and Middlesbrough are adjacent towns on the River Tees some ten miles from the sea. Stockton is on the County Durham side, north and west of Middlesbrough, which is on the Yorkshire side. The River Tees has been recognised as the northern boundary of Yorkshire since the time of the Danes in the ninth century, and for the purposes of this book I shall pay only minimal attention to the local government provisions of the last thirty or so years - our history makes us what we are. For a fuller understanding, it is also important to say where Middlesbrough and Stockton are not, in particular that at 35 miles distant they are not on or near the River Tyne, nor are their people Geordies. The particular accent of the general population has a distinctive quality which comes from its being an amalgam of Durham and Yorkshire.

Those who move to live in Tees-side often say how pleasantly surprised they were upon coming here. They enthuse about the beauty of the North Yorkshire Moors National Park, and how easy it is to get to (by car, that is). They comment on the wonders of Whitby and York, of Durham and Upper Teesdale, of Ripon and Fountains Abbey and of the delightful countryside to be found throughout the region. After a few minutes you realise that they are saying that the good thing about living in Middlesbrough or Stockton is that it is easy to get away from! In the years of its greatest success, the area was a seething mass of iron and steel works, furnaces, rolling mills, slag heaps and marshalling yards. Here were the greatest bridge builders in the world, as well as many shipbuilding yards and, later, oil rigs. There were also huge chemical plants and oil refineries with their pipes, retorts, tanks and chimneys, creating an industrial chemical complex greater than any in Europe. All these covered the district in the smoke, grit and fumes which were an inevitable consequence of its achievements. Nowadays much of the industry has declined, though what remains is still impressive. There is no shortage of schemes to revitalise the area, and much has already been achieved. Nevertheless a heritage of such down-to-earth quality leaves little room for finesse, and the growth of cultural and academic achievement is an uphill struggle here. The creation of the University of Teesside, and of Durham's University College Stockton (in Thornaby) have been welcome steps in recent years, where hitherto this could boast only of being the largest urban area without a university.

Stockton-on-Tees is well known as the birthplace of railways. Here on 27th September 1825 the Stockton and Darlington company started the world's first public steam railway. It is an ancient town dating back at least to the twelfth century, and although its castle was demolished in 1652, it has continued to flourish as a market town serving an extensive rural area. Prior to the development of Middlesbrough it was the established port on the River Tees, and it continued as an important centre of shipbuilding. The present parish church was built in 1712 and the wide and gracious High Street dates from the same period. The race course was there by 1746, the first bridge to what is now Thornaby in 1771, and two cuts which were made in the meandering River Tees in 1810 and 1831 considerably shortened the distance to be traversed from the port to the North Sea.

The object of the new railway in 1825 was the shipment of coal, to which end a new terminal was constructed a few miles downstream in 1830. This was Middlesbrough, a tiny settlement in bleak and marshy territory. The "infant Hercules" of Gladstone's 1862 speech grew to 100,000 by 1900, thereby achieving a distinctive status as the fastest growing town of them all, in an age and nation characterised by huge industrial expansion. This growth had been stimulated by the discovery of iron ore in the nearby Cleveland hills in 1850, with Middlesbrough the ideal site for what became a great iron and steel industry. In

The Transporter bridge over the River Tees was opened in 1911 and is here viewed from Port Clarence. The church spire is St Hilda's in old Middlesbrough.

Victorian times the very speed of the town's growth was greater than could be coped with, and conditions were often chaotic, the local folk memory subsequently painting a picture of circumstances not unlike the American wild west.

The American influence here has been remarkably strong and persistent, more so than in Britain as a whole. Transport examples are to be found in the more recent names. Unlike Americans, we use the word 'municipal' simply as an adjective, not as part of a title, but here the 1968 bus undertaking uniquely did so under the name Teesside Municipal Transport. With the changes under the new Cleveland County in 1974 things went even further. Again in a manner unique in Britain the new local authorities appropriated the name of the operator in Cleveland, Ohio, with the title Cleveland Transit.

What Tees-side may have lacked in some respects, it made up for in vitality, and this was as noticeable in local transport as it was in any other sphere. As the nineteenth century was coming to a close, a horse tramway in Middlesbrough and a steam tramway in Stockton were struggling to survive. Journeys between Stockton and Middlesbrough, a distance of only four miles, were particularly awkward. The topography of the railways was ill suited to such journeys, for which you would

have been best advised to walk or take the steam tram to Thornaby station for your train to Middlesbrough. The usual, because cheaper, alternative was to travel by ferry boat from Stockton, on an unreliable service beset by the tides and by other river traffic, to Newport and to take the horse tram from there into town. Then in 1898 the Imperial Tramways Company commenced a five-minute electric tram service between the two towns, and a new era was born. The name "Tees-side" came into use at about this time, and it could justly be said that the tramways created it. The undertaking was at the very pinnacle of British tramway achievement at this date - it was the first major system to be worked entirely by large bogie cars, providing a steadier ride and a larger capacity than had hitherto been available anywhere else. A hundred years later the route remains the backbone of the local bus network and is still known colloquially as "the main line", and even more colloquially as "the drag".

A fundamental consequence of the provision of transport facilities is that places are effectively brought together, and as more and more people travel between them, the age-old isolation of individual towns gradually dissolves. There are many respects in which the past century has seen widespread use of the name Tees-side, more recently without the hyphen, to denote this identifiable homogeneous urban and industrial region without differentiating one local town from another; one such example is Teesside International Airport, which in modern terms actually lies partly in the Borough of Darlington to the west. Nevertheless, I have chosen to give this book the title "Middlesbrough & Stockton" rather than "Tees-side", because these towns remain distinctly different from each other, and their transport history reflects this strongly. This feature should not be glossed over, and the region should not be presented as a seamless whole. In this it more closely resembles Arnold Bennett's "Five Towns" of the Potteries than any more readily identifiable large city. Of particular additional significance in the municipal transport story are the Borough of Thornaby-on-Tees (between Middlesbrough and Stockton) and the Eston Urban District (east of Middlesbrough), as will be seen. Nowadays Middlesbrough is the effective 'capital', but the area developed piecemeal, rather than growing uniformly outwards from a single focal point. There is considerable local rivalry between Middlesbrough and Stockton, and various developments in Middlesbrough's favour continue to cause ill feeling of the "we've been sold down the river" variety in Stockton. More significantly but unobtrusively, in today's highly integrated bus service network, where most parts of Stockton have a through bus to most parts of Middlesbrough, the vast majority of passenger journeys are simply to and from "town". If you live in Stockton, that means Stockton, and correspondingly in Middlesbrough. Each town serves separately as a focus for a number of places a little further afield, with Thornaby, Billingham and Yarm naturally tending towards Stockton (and nowadays also part of it administratively whilst remaining distinctly separate places). To the east and south, places such as Eston, South Bank, Grangetown and Nunthorpe have Middlesbrough as their natural focal point, though of course all the local districts have much self contained activity and much very immediate local passenger traffic on the buses. This is especially so in Billingham.

The towns of Hartlepool and West Hartlepool, on the coast some ten miles to the north, were merged under the Hartlepool name in 1967. They have never been regarded as part of Tees-side, but West Hartlepool's buses and their Hartlepool successors have operated to Middlesbrough since 1921. The word "to" does not always mean "into", because for many years

they did not cross the Tees but stopped short at Port Clarence, and passengers reached the town by using Middlesbrough Corporation's Transporter Bridge. This was operated by the Transport Department from 1936, and in a remarkable instance of succession is now run by Stagecoach. It is unlikely that there is anywhere else where the passenger is issued with a Stagecoach ticket marked "Pedestrian".

At the end of the twentieth century and the beginning of the twenty-first, the very idea of municipal buses has slipped away from popular thought. Buses belong to companies, who run them for profit, and the public purse supports them only through a tendering process in situations where necessary journeys are unremunerative. Even the few remaining council-owned undertakings are nowadays constituted as companies, and have to survive on the open market. It was not always so. Within the easy memory of many is a regulated period when almost every sizeable council in an urban area ran its own trams and buses for the benefit of its citizens. A marginal profit enabled an undertaking to run without being a drain on the rates, but where necessary the rates would support the service. In the 1970s this assistance grew alarmingly, which led before long to the downfall not only of the municipal bus undertakings but of the very notion of public service on which they were founded.

That idea of public service was very much to the forefront in the years from about 1916. The Act of Parliament under which the Imperial company had built the electric tramways in Middlesbrough, Thornaby and Stockton made provision for compulsory purchase by the corporations after 21 years, which period would elapse by 1918. There was much dissatisfaction that the Bristol-based company was making significant profits at the expense of local people whilst the standard of service declined and the profits were not reinvested in the area. Meanwhile the company perceived the compulsory purchase to be a foregone conclusion (as indeed it proved to be), and was in consequence unwilling to spend money which it felt it could not recoup. Nevertheless it strove to protect its interests from competitors by introducing motor bus services in 1914, but soon afterwards was faced with the restrictions and burdens of wartime. The municipal intentions to purchase the undertaking were duly announced, but agreement with the company about the price to be paid could not be reached, and the case had to go to arbitration.

The corporations also had to agree how they were going to operate their respective shares of the system. Stockton and Thornaby wanted a joint board to run a single undertaking, but Middlesbrough insisted on having its own separate service. "Tees-side" was a reality only up to a point.

The Imperial company's undertaking therefore effectively split into two when the corporations took over in 1921, with Thornaby and Stockton forming their own joint tramways committee and retaining the company's red livery. The joint tramways were managed by Stockton Corporation until Thornaby withdrew in 1930, having done nothing in the meantime except own nine trams with its share of the through service. Stockton also did nothing of note with the tramway, but did develop the motor bus service. This took over from the trams on New Year's Day 1932.

The story at Middlesbrough was at first strikingly different. A new livery of dark blue and cream was introduced, nine new top-covered double deck trams were purchased, an impressive new depot was constructed and extensive track repairs and other improvements were put in hand. This long-hoped-for publicly owned service thus began with a flourish and with high hopes, but those postwar years of unforeseeable serious economic difficulty did not provide the right climate for such a venture. This can be illustrated by the case of the Sunday trams which the company, despite municipal pressure, had ceased to operate in the final year because of serious coal shortages affecting their Stockton power station. Local firms were operating a charabanc service instead. When the corporations took over, they too found themselves facing the same problems, and then it was their turn not to operate Sunday trams, at least until the situation eased. As at Stockton, the motor bus service in Middlesbrough was also developed, and the remaining tramway came to the same sorry end only a few years after that of Stockton.

A peculiar matter of detail from this period reveals a strange contrast between the high ideals of public ownership and service on the one hand, and an untidy carelessness on the other. This was the renumbering of the tram fleets, a consequence of the way that the Imperial cars had been distributed by lot among the three corporations. From the neat group of cars numbered from 1 to 60 emerged two fleets with randomly scattered numbers. At first they all looked the same, in the Imperial's by now faded red and white livery, and carrying the company's title in large letters. The obvious need to distinguish who owned which car was accentuated by the initial need to stable some of Middlesbrough's fleet at the Stockton depot. You would expect in these circumstances, with the authorities having had long notice of the event, that the affected cars would have been renumbered overnight. Middlesbrough had decided to have its trams numbered from 100 upwards, and Stockton and Thornaby together had chosen to use the numbers 1 to 29. In the event, Middlesbrough took eighteen months even to clear the spaces in the range 1 to 29, and was almost certainly pushed repeatedly by Stockton even to do that much. As Middlesbrough had taken all the single deckers, it was with the open top double deckers that it might have been expected that repainting into its new dark blue livery would also have been a priority. Not at all! Their repainting was spread out over at least seven years, and it seems that in a period of over ten years of joint operation with Stockton and Thornaby some cars were never repainted blue at all, and at least one was never renumbered.

Municipal enthusiasm to operate public transport services had meanwhile made remarkable progress elsewhere in the district. Proposals to extend the Imperial's tramway eastwards came to nothing in themselves, but led to further proposals for a 'track-less tram' service - using what since the 1930s have universally been described as trolleybuses. During the preparatory period, this private venture was taken over jointly by Eston and Middlesbrough councils, and the system opened in 1919 as the first municipal operation in the area under the name of the Tees-side Railless Traction Board. Ownership was in the proportions of two-thirds and one-third respectively. Starting from a point a short distance beyond the tram terminus, the wires linked North Ormesby (in Middlesbrough) with South Bank, Grangetown and Normanby (all in Eston Urban District), and served an area of intense industrial activity in iron and steel manufacture and shipbuilding. The TRTB undertaking was noteworthy in its early days for a unique petrol-trolleybus, and at the end for opening Britain's final trolleybus route extension before being the second-last system to close.

Middlesbrough Corporation was thus in the ironic situation of successfully participating in a joint transport board with Eston whilst

Stockton-on-Tees Corporation
Tramways.

Thornaby-on-Tees Corporation
Tramways.

CONTROLLED AND WORKED
BY A JOINT COMMITTEE OF
THE TWO CORPORATIONS

RULES & REGULATIONS

FOR

EMPLOYEES.

MAY, 1922.

STOCKTON-ON-TEES:
COATES & CO. (PRINTERS) LTD., WHARF STREET.
1922.

*Above left and centre: A variety of destination and route letter blinds from Middlesbrough Corporation; the destination blind is of the style current from 1945 to 1953 and is very similar to the standard style of 1934-9. (A Wood) **Above right:** Thornaby Corporation's involvement is illustrated by the title page of the 1922 rule book. **Below:** A Tees-side Railless Traction Board window bill.*

CHRISTMAS DAY, Dec. 25th, 1936.

For the convenience of Workmen on the early shifts Additional Cars will be run before advertised service commences at 8-15 a.m., as under, AT ORDINARY FARES ONLY :—

Depart from North Ormesby	Depart from Grangetown	Depart from Normanby
5-34 a.m. for Grangetown	5-36 a.m. to North Ormesby	5-30 a.m. to North Ormesby
5-49 ,, ,, ,,	5-53 ,, ,, South Bank	7-0 ,, ,, ,, ,,
5-53 ,, ,, Depot only	6-10 ,, ,, North Ormesby	7-44 ,, ,, ,, ,,
6-41 ,, ,, Normanby	7-11 ,, ,, ,, ,,	
6-54 ,, ,, Grangetown	7-18 ,, ,, ,, ,,	
7-0 ,, ,, ,,	7-36 ,, ,, ,, ,,	
7-18 ,, ,, ,,		
7-49 ,, ,, ,,		
7-54 ,, ,, NORMANBY		

C. W. F. COZENS,
General Manager.

December, 22nd, 1936.

adamantly refusing to enter into a similar arrangement with Stockton and Thornaby. By running its own separate transport department it also had the distinction of operating two unconnected undertakings. Both Stockton and the TRTB buses ran extensively in Middlesbrough, but the TRTB was there in its own right, whereas Stockton gained access only by virtue of joint services with Middlesbrough. The irony of this was that Middlesbrough operated several joint services with Stockton, with whom it refused to enter a joint board, whilst operating nothing jointly with the TRTB despite the degree of common ownership. Only in the final period before the eventual amalgamation in 1968 were serious proposals put forward for a joint Eston-Stockton service involving all three.

In the principal period from the Road Traffic Act 1930 until that amalgamation, the three undertakings all prospered, and each had a distinctive character, beginning with what you would see upon first acquaintance. The Board's vehicles operated in a restrained dark green livery well suited to an area of heavy industry. The fleetname was presented in the form of a stylish Maltese cross. For twenty five years Stockton's fleet used the red livery inherited from the Imperial company, but it gave way to a mid-green from 1947. Middlesbrough's dark blue had a partially unpainted version for some years, until the arrival of manager Frank Lythgoe in 1934. He was far and away the most prominent character in the whole of municipal transport operation in Tees-side, transforming the finances of his undertaking, and repainting the fleet in a rich deep blue version of the style he had previously used at Rawtenstall. Although all three operators' vehicles were well maintained and presented a smart appearance, under Lythgoe Middlesbrough's had a touch of class which the others never quite achieved. Despite the chagrin of the advertising contractor and the misgivings of his Committee, Frank Lythgoe dispensed with exterior advertisements by 1939, arguing that the smart appearance of the fleet would draw passengers, and therefore revenue, more successfully than advertisements. Subsequently Stockton also gave up exterior advertising, perhaps in connection with the new green livery. The question did not concern the Tees-side Railless Traction Board to the same degree, because they did not operate any double deckers until 1941, and their advertisements never extended beyond the rear panels of single deckers. In any event, after the end of the second world war in 1945, none of the three operators' vehicles carried external advertisements, and Middlesbrough's and Stockton's displayed their town coat-of-arms on the upper panels. Given the ubiquity of advertising, it was quite remarkable that three adjacent municipal operators should all refrain from it. Stockton saw an opportunity to create a decorated Christmas bus in 1947, in a style which would have been quite inconsistent with the display of advertisements. It became a strong and distinctive local tradition of which vestiges remain over fifty years later.

Frank Lythgoe retired with due honour in 1964, and Middlesbrough's prevailing standards gradually declined. This was only a harbinger of what was to come. The 1968 merger of local authorities in the region was one of several trial schemes leading ultimately to that which affected the whole of England and Wales in 1974. In this case, Middlesbrough, Stockton and Eston were three of six authorities merged into the new County Borough of Teesside on 1st April 1968. This automatically put the three municipal bus operators under a common ownership, so that in the end the amalgamation was not decided on the basis of transport operation at all, but on the wider one of local government itself. Thus was created Teesside Municipal Transport, with a weak turquoise livery based on compromise rather than quality. The mixture of blue and green was perceived as demonstrating continuity with what had gone before whilst avoiding the impression that any one operator had taken over the other two. In an economic climate of unexpected difficulty, the new undertaking was quickly in trouble. Staff shortages and rapidly increasing traffic congestion played havoc with service reliability, and frequent large fare increases were only slightly restrained by the appearance of external advertisements. The fact that the combined fleet was not renumbered into a single series for $2^1/_2$ years was a strange echo of Middlesbrough's similar lethargy of the 1920s. In the meantime many fleet numbers existed in triplicate. No such lethargy affected the repainting of vehicles into the turquoise livery. Indeed, each of the three undertakings to be absorbed had already started such repainting up to eighteen months before the merger took place, but each used a slightly different shade of paint from the others, and it seemed to be Stockton's that was eventually adopted by TMT itself. The undertaking was faced with the task of integrating three disparate organisations, including one with trolleybuses, and creating a fully integrated network of services. That these things were achieved at all is greatly to the credit of a management team working in almost impossible circumstances. It was inevitable that standards of presentation slipped, with buses frequently running with the odd unpainted panel after an accident, many buses having destination blinds that did not fit the boxes, and others having three track number blinds fitted in off-centre positions that were not at all easy on the eye. The new 'Letraset' style of bus stop sign made an early appearance here in 1971. In the works areas they quickly got very grimy. It was noticeable that alterations to the numbers shown on the signs were usually made merely by amending the appropriate little square, with a dab of white paint and the new number stuck over it. It was nobody's job to clean the rest of the plate. Somehow that typified the untidiness of the immediate area - the whole nation depended on the industrial activity, but its grime was too pervasive to be overcome.

Things had improved significantly by the time of the next reorganisation of local government, which occurred in 1974. This created the county of Cleveland and three new boroughs on Teesside. The appropriation of the almost forgotten historic name of Langbaurgh gave a new identity to Eston and a large area to the east including Redcar, whilst Stockton and Middlesbrough were once more their own distinct, if expanded, selves. All three had powers to run their own bus services, but unlike the situation in 1921, all three chose to create a joint board to operate the existing unified undertaking under the name of Cleveland Transit. A new, stronger and more positive green and yellow livery was adopted, symbolic of the progress that would be made in the years ahead. This enterprise still exists, much changed, as a subsidiary of Stagecoach Holdings plc, but its history from 1974 is beyond the scope of this book.

In compiling this presentation, I am grateful to many people who have had a hand in it, making possible many improvements which have contributed to the finished result. Series editor John Banks and long-term observers Ron Maybray, John D Watson and Andy Wood have been particularly helpful. Unlike some of them, your author is not a native of the district, and accordingly has had more to learn. For the photographs, those not from my own camera are individually acknowledged. Like most other volumes in this series, this work is not intended to be either a history or a fleet list, but a visual presentation. As you sit in your armchair and browse through these pictures, evoking a previous age which is not so very far away, let them take you on a ramble through town centres, heavy industrial areas, pleasant suburbs and burgeoning new housing areas. As you do so, remember Lady Florence Bell who in 1907 charted the daily lives of the people of the iron and steel works of Middlesbrough in her classic book "At The Works". It conveys an understanding of why Tees-side is as it is. Join its people in their journeys over the years, to work, to the shops, to the cinema and pub, and back home again. I trust you will find it enjoyable and rewarding.

Philip Battersby,
Middlesbrough,
June 2001

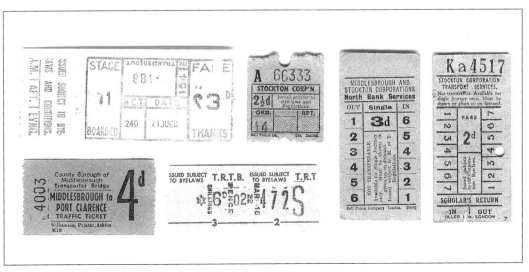

Above: Although it had already received advertisements, the Imperial Tramways Company's Milnes-built car No. **26** of 1898 was still new enough for there to be quite a sense of occasion when this picture was taken at the terminus in The Crescent, Middlesbrough. The bicycle too was still a recent invention at that time. The tram subsequently became Stockton Corporation's 26 and was scrapped in 1932, but the wall is still there. *(Author's Collection)*

Below: Another wall still partly in existence identifies the location of this view in Marton Road, Middlesbrough, of the Company's Bristol C65 bus No. **64** (**AE 3198**) early in 1914. It was re-registered locally as DC440, probably before entering service, and also passed to Stockton Corporation in 1921. *(M J Tozer Collection)*

Municipal transport in the area commenced in November 1919 with ten trackless trams, as they were then known, of the Tees-side Railless Traction Board. They were supplied by Railless Ltd, with chassis by the Cleveland Car Company, Darlington, and bodies by English Electric. Numbered 1 to 10, they received registration numbers under revised legislation in 1921. In that year, on the NER bridge over the Eston branch, No. **9** (**AJ 5864**) passes new Roe-bodied Straker-Clough No. **17** (**AJ 7513**). *(Author's Collection)*

Above: Middlesbrough Corporation Tramways purchased six Dodson-bodied AEC YC-type buses in anticipation of the start of its operations in April 1921. One of them, registered **DC 805** but fleet number unknown, was pictured at the Port Clarence side of the Transporter bridge on the service to Seaton Carew run jointly with West Hartlepool Corporation. The crew outnumber the passengers at this bleak spot, and the solid tyres seem to have suffered a lot of wear and tear. *(Author's Collection)*

Below: A fulsome display of municipal pride was the order of the day on 10th November 1921 when Middlesbrough's Tramways Committee took delivery of the first completed new car (No. **135**) from Hurst, Nelson of Motherwell. The new depot in Parliament Road was under construction at the time. This is one of several large mounted pictures commissioned to mark the occasion. *(Author's Collection)*

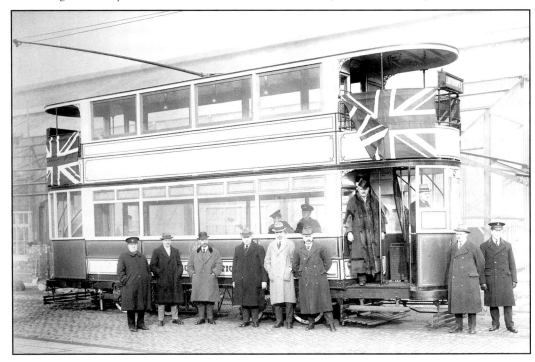

Above: Middlesbrough's No. **82** (**DC 4142**) was a 14-seater built on a Ford T chassis by local coachbuilder W G Edmond in 1923. It too is on the Seaton Carew service, and stands in the station yard at Port Clarence. *(Edmond & Milburn Ltd)*

Below: Stockton Corporation also commenced its purchases for 1921 with AEC single deckers, but soon settled down to become a strong Leyland customer throughout the 1920s. This Leyland-bodied A13 model of 1924 was numbered **16**, and had a blind reading "Fairfield" although it was yet to receive its PT3386 registration plate. *(Senior Transport Archive/BCVM)*

Above: The petrol-electric trolleybus which could operate beyond the wires by use of the petrol engine was delivered to the TRTB in 1924. The vehicle was excitedly reported in the trade press of the day, but remained unique among British operators. In this view, Roe-bodied No. **22** (**PY 1845**) displays its licence disc, but is probably on trial before entering service. *(Senior Transport Archive)*

Below: It was 1926 when the Board took delivery of its first conventional petrol bus. The picture of Daimler CM No. **23** (**PY 5573**) was taken outside the Roe coach works in Leeds. *(Senior Transport Archive)*

Above and >>> *next page upper:* An early example of one-man operation was Stockton's Leyland Lioness No. **28** (**UP 209**) of 1927. The folding door is seen in the open position from outside. The evocative interior view shows a rather solemn demonstration of the closing operation requiring the use of a suitably placed handle. The body was also by Leyland, with the pictures taken before delivery. *(Both: Senior Transport Archive/BCVM)*

Below: Stockton was an early and enthusiastic customer for the Leyland Titan TD1, commencing with six in 1928. In this official view, No. **35** (**UP 1541**) is strangely posed, probably on Norton Road. Any thoughts that the occupants of the bus might have been press-ganged office staff are dispelled by the interest they were showing in the photographer, and the mixture of people which included a mother and baby in the front seat. The bus was operating route 2 to Yarm. *(Senior Transport Archive/BCVM)*

Above: Coachbuilder W G Edmond had several pictures taken of the Leyland PLSC3 Lions he bodied for Middlesbrough in 1928, and they are far superior to known views of the type in service. This one is probably outside the town's Albert Park. Note the leather splash guard - its use was soon discontinued. *(Edmond & Milburn Ltd)*

Below: The superior "big city" image was brought to Middlesbrough by three Guy-bodied Guy six-wheelers in 1929, which were the Corporation's first double deck buses. In this busy scene at the town's Exchange bus station, the unpainted livery of No. **63** (**DC 8929**) is well displayed. The picture also introduces us to Middlesbrough's distinctive route letters. *(Author's Collection)*

Above: In another example of an official photograph excelling any known view of the vehicle in service, we see one of Stockton's several 1930 trial purchases, AEC Regal 4 No. **12** (**UP 4744**). The body was built by Brush of Loughborough. Further house-building soon rendered the destination "Gainford Road" obsolete.

Below: After Stockton had made further trial purchases, fleets of Daimler double deckers replaced the joint Middlesbrough and Stockton tram service on New Year's Day 1932. In preference to yet another official view, here is a picture postcard of Stockton's No. **58** (**UP 5326**), a CG6 with Brush body, albeit on the Yarm service. In this busy market day scene in the town's High Street, the previously mentioned Leyland Lioness No. **28** (**UP 209**) stands alongside. *(Both: Author's Collection)*

Above: Middlesbrough Corporation used several body builders for its 1931 tram replacement CH6 Daimlers, and the one shown here on No. **59** (**XG 736**) was by Hoyal. This official photograph shows an open-top tram inside the depot, but is the more remarkable for the way that the print was marked up for the benefit of the advertising contractors, Griffiths & Millington of London. *(Author's Collection)*

Below: There is no one in sight in this picture inside the Linthorpe Carriage Works of W G Edmond, and yet the scene is a hive of activity! Some of a batch of six CH6 Daimlers for Middlesbrough Corporation are seen under construction in 1932 , with No. **46** (**XG 1389**) nearest the camera. *(Edmond & Milburn Ltd)*

Above: Other new vehicles in 1932 were eight trolleybuses for the Tees-side Railless system. They replaced the survivors of the original ten of 1919, and the opportunity was taken to photograph the old and the new number 1 together. The new vehicles had chassis and bodies by Ransomes, Sims and Jefferies of Ipswich. *(Author's Collection)*

Below: The Great Yorkshire Show was held in Middlesbrough in July 1933 and the Corporation judiciously augmented its bus fleet with several Daimler demonstrators which helped to deal with the crowds. Here are two of them in a busy scene at the Exchange, probably collecting passengers who had just arrived by train. In front is **VC 8351**, a lowbridge Hoyal-bodied CH6 in Birmingham Corporation dark blue livery. Note the extraordinary emergency exit upstairs on the nearside. *(Author's Collection)*

Above: A Daimler demonstrator which was subsequently taken into stock by Middlesbrough as No. **23** was **VK 3418**, by then to CP6 specification and with highbridge Hoyal body. It features on the right in this view inside Parliament Road depot, Middlesbrough, taken after the 1934 departure of the remaining trams. Nearer the centre of the picture are four of the lowbridge Leyland TD3c Titans that had replaced them. *(Author's Collection)*

Below: The lower saloon of the first of that batch, No. **26** (**XG 2327**), was photographed before delivery. The two single seats at the front are particularly noteworthy. *(Senior Transport Archive)*

Above: In the same year, 1934, Stockton added further highbridge Daimlers. This excellent Brush official view of No. **18** (**UP 9153**), a CP6, shows what great advances in styling were being made at this time. *(Senior Transport Archive)*

Below: By 1936 manager Frank Lythgoe was taking his first new deliveries at Middlesbrough. This well proportioned Roe-bodied Leyland TD4c, No. **67** (**XG 4257**), shows the stunning effect of the new rich blue livery with black, gold and blue lining. Even though slightly amended twenty years later, this livery remained essentially characteristic of the undertaking until just before the amalgamation of 1968. *(Senior Transport Archive)*

Although the two views on this page are no more than amateur snapshots, they illustrate the beginnings of Stockton Corporation's long tradition of decorated buses. The jubilee of King George V in 1935 was marked by the adorning of the newest bus, Weymann-bodied Daimler COG5 No. **21** (**UP 9156**). The 1936 batch had Cravens bodies, and one of them, No.**15** (**BPT 786**), was chosen to commemorate the coronation of King George VI in May 1937. Looking back at these buses after 65 years, it is hard to realise that the two views bridge the huge crisis of the abdication of Edward VIII in 1936. *(Both: Author's Collection)*

Above: Five new trolleybuses for the TRTB in 1936 replaced the Strakers and the unique petrol-electric vehicle. They were Massey-bodied Leylands Nos 9-13 (VN9434-8). Number **9** took a dive off the railway bridge at South Bank in August 1941, and whilst the staff wondered what to do, a crowd of urchins gathered to enjoy the sport. It took two days to get the bus out of its predicament. *(Author's Collection)*

Below: The last petrol-engined bus new to the TRTB came in May 1938 as No. **24** (**APY 557**). This was a Leyland LT9 Lion, a type often mistaken for a TS8 Tiger because this final model of the four-cylinder Lion range had the Tiger style of radiator. Number 24 was latterly much photographed, but usually from the front, so here is the official rear view. *(Senior Transport Archive/BCVM)*

Above: Harold Franklin ran "Panther Services" from Middlesbrough to the outlying village of Seamer, but sold out to Middlesbrough Corporation who took over on 1st January 1939. Edmond-bodied Bedford **XG 5886** was one of two vehicles to pass to the Corporation during a period when the fleet was rapidly becoming entirely double-decked. The result was a residual need for two single-deckers which marked the next thirty years.

Below: The other ex-Panther vehicle was a much older Chevrolet registered **DC9253**. This drastic accident in Longford Street, Middlesbrough, only eight weeks after the takeover, brought its running days to an end, despite the fact that it had been repainted in fleet livery and numbered **2**. The Bedford was number 1. *(Edmond & Milburn Ltd; Author's Collection)*

Above: In the immediate prewar years, Middlesbrough had built up a substantial fleet of torque converter Leyland Titans with highbridge bodies by Eastern Coach Works. Number **92** (**XG 7497**) was one of the last batch of this combination, delivered in 1940. In this quiet but typical scene at the Exchange in postwar days, it is parked between special duties. The display "North Ormesby 11" was extensively used on works specials between Billingham and Middlesbrough, and is also shown on the bus behind, 1945 Guy No. **19** (**XG 8041**). *(D F Parker Collection)*

Below: The TRTB received some very similar vehicles in 1941, although the bodies were by Roe and the transmission was conventional clutch and gearbox. They were the Board's first double-deckers. This one is No. **27** (**BVN 234**), seen in postwar days in the depot yard and also screened up for North Ormesby, which in this case it would approach from the east. *(Author's Collection)*

Right: The TRTB's first tower dated from 1912 and came on a Halley chassis from Sheffield Corporation in 1921. The chassis was replaced by another Halley in 1925 and the whole withdrawn in 1941. The new tower built in that year was mounted on 1930 Leyland LT2 Lion **VN 1962**, which had been bus number 25. In October 1953 it was photographed near Grangetown with the crew preparing to lift a redundant pole. *(J C Gillham)*

Below: Stockton Corporation received two unfrozen Leylands in 1942. This one, No. **84** (**EUP 862**) had Leyland lowbridge bodywork and was being checked and sent off by an inspector in Church Road, Stockton, one Saturday in November 1956. The destination was the football ground at Ayresome Park, Middlesbrough. The author craves your indulgence for this one - it was his first ever photograph.

Above: One new trolleybus for the TRTB also came in 1942, Sunbeam MF2A No. **14** (**BVN 694**) with East Lancashire body. In this posed view on Normanby Road the wartime white trim and masked headlamps are apparent. Note also the colour route light mounted to the right of the destination box. *(Author's Collection)*

Below: In 1944 and 1945 the Board received its first double-deck trolleybuses, eight Sunbeam W models whose chassis lasted until 1971. In a typical scene in Grangetown Square in the early postwar period, morning shoppers board Weymann-bodied No. **17** (**CPY 288**). The conductress carries her TIM machine, and the photographer is an obvious "focus" of attention. *(Author's Collection)*

Above: Stockton Corporation received a considerable number of wartime utility buses. The first of them was No. **86** (**FPT 353**), a Duple-bodied Daimler CWA6 of 1943, seen here in the early 1950s, and which continued to work into the town after sale to Transport Motor Services (Bishop Auckland) Ltd. The cramped depot yard was to retain its tramway atmosphere until the move to new premises in 1965. *(Author's Collection)*

Below: Even the wartime grey livery was capable of being the basis of a Stockton Corporation decorated bus. This one is No. **91** (**FPT 468**), with white trim to aid visibility in the blackout, masked headlamps, and a Home Guard driver in military uniform. It was a 1944 Brush-bodied CWA6, and carried various royal motifs, but did not announce any particular occasion or event. *(Author's Collection)*

Above: Stockton's spacious High Street, venue of the twice-weekly market from time immemorial, appears to advantage on many picture postcards but rarely does so on bus enthusiasts' photographs. This view of the Town Hall is taken from an original glass negative dating from the winter of 1945-46. Its speciality is Glasgow Corporation's No. **416 (YS 2062)**, a 1935 Cowieson-bodied Leyland TD4 which was one of several briefly on hire to Stockton Corporation. Several of Stockton's own buses appear in the distance. *(Author's Collection)*

Below: Another wartime expedient in 1945 was the building of new bodies for some of Middlesbrough Corporation's 1934 Leylands. The manufacturer was Northern Coachbuilders of Newcastle. The first of the type, **XG 2327**, had been renumbered from 26 to **36** by the time of this picture at the Exchange, and it lasted until 1951. *(Roy Marshall)*

Above: One of Middlesbrough's fascinating peculiarities was the inclusion of flat fares on the route letter blind. In this scene in Stockton High Street, the 1945 wartime Guy with Northern Counties body is No. **16** (**XG 7999**). The destination "Special, Fare 4d" suggests football or greyhound racing, and it appears that all the passengers are men. *(Author's collection)*

Below: Another 1945 utility bus was Stockton Corporation's No. **103** (**FUP 254**). This was a Strachans-bodied Guy Arab, working on the 8 service without being able to display the number. On a busy market day, it was probably a duplicate. *(Author's collection)*

Above: When postwar deliveries reverted to peacetime standards, Stockton Corporation received a variety of buses with Massey bodies. The Guy version included No. **106 (GUP 558)**, which arrived during the cataclysmic three months' snow early in 1947. At the end of the year 106 was decorated for Christmas. With hindsight the decorations seem almost glum, but in those austere years the Christmas bus would bring cheer to many and the crew certainly seem to have been in the spirit of things. *(Author's collection)*

Below: Another duplicate seen at the north end of Stockton High Street was being worked by one of the more distinctive of the town's buses, a 1947 Massey-bodied Bristol K6G. This is No. **9 (HPT 430)**, ready to run to Blandford's Corner, a convenient turning point for short workings along Norton Road. *(R A Stone)*

Above: Middlesbrough's single deck requirement had become a problem by 1945, which was solved the following year by the receipt of a Guy and a Leyland from the Roe coach factory. The Guy was No. 3 (**XG 8360**), much better known in later years as No. **100**. In this picture dating from the early 1960s and taken at the Exchange bus stand, it is ready to work its usual run, the ex-Panther route to Seamer with its alliterative service letter. *(R A Stone)*

Below: Middlesbrough reverted to purchasing Leyland buses for several years after the war, and PD1A No. **50** (**XG 9302**) delivered in 1947 had a Northern Counties lowbridge body. A typical duty in the late 1950s included shoppers' duplicates between Middlesbrough and Stockton Town Halls. Rather than be idle on half-closing day, passengers would go to Stockton market on Wednesdays and to Middlesbrough's shops on Thursdays. Here the bus loads in Stockton on such a duty. *(R H G Simpson)*

In 1947 the Tees-side Railless Traction Board was the proud recipient of new all-Leyland PD1A buses. The vehicles are exemplified here by No. **36** (**DVN 633**) photographed before delivery. The distinctive destination blinds for the Board's motor bus services had a green background instead of black, and the route letters (they used S and T) were yellow instead of white. *(Author's collection/BCVM)*

Above: A substantial batch which looked like more of the same was added to the TRTB fleet in 1949, but they were on the PD2/1 chassis. The Board's Middlesbrough service had terminated for some years at Queen's Square near the railway station, and then at the Exchange, but from 1950 gained better access to the principal shopping and business area with a stop at the Town Hall and a terminus in Borough Road. This view shows No. **47 (FAJ 497)** at the Town Hall. *(R F Mack)*

Below: Nineteen-fifty at TRTB saw seven Sunbeam trolleybuses with East Lancashire bodies delivered from the Bridlington factory. The depot was in South Bank, in the strangely-named Cargo Fleet locality, indicated on the screen in this picture. This view shows No. **1 (GAJ 11)** in the later, simplified, livery with the whole of the top deck in unrelieved green. *(Photomatic)*

Above: In advance of the general relaxation of the width limit, Stockton Corporation received twelve eight-feet-wide Leyland PD2/3 Titans with Leyland bodies in 1949. They are understood to have been a diverted South African order. They worked the intensive joint 0 service for many years, as depicted here with No. **116** (**JUP 151**) loading in Stockton for Middlesbrough. *(Author's collection)*

Below: Several of the same batch were extensively rebuilt by the Corporation in 1961/2, and the process changed the appearance considerably. Compare this view of rebuilt No. **113** (**JUP 148**) with 116 above. Service 6 from Thornaby through Stockton to Norton carried much local traffic despite being covered for most of its length by the very frequent 0 service. *(John Heighway)*

Above: In 1949 Middlesbrough Corporation returned to the Leyland and Eastern Coach Works combination, but the designs were very different from prewar and the PD1/3 chassis was eight feet wide. In a scene at the Exchange, No. **62 (ADC 662)** waits to leave for Billingham on the 11 service worked jointly with Stockton. '11' was the only number among Middlesbrough's distinctive route letters. *(Ron Maybray)*

Below: From the same coachbuilder, but in markedly different proportions, were sixteen Guy Arabs delivered to Middlesbrough in 1950. In a pleasant suburban scene at Roman Road in September 1965, No. **82 (AXG 682)** operates the T service, which was entirely separate from the TRTB's T service even though both could be seen together in the town centre. The destination 'Tollesby' demonstrates the stylish lettering in which all curves were circles or parts of circles.

Above: The Gothic splendour of Middlesbrough Town Hall, completed in 1888, and the stylish lines of Stockton Corporation's Massey-bodied Leyland PD2/3 No. **68** (**KPT 773**) of 1949, enhanced each other. The bus was operating the Middlesbrough - Stockton via Acklam service, also joint and also numbered 11. This strange quirk was the result of dividing a previous service into two but not renumbering either section. *(S N J White)*

Below: The 25 Stockton Massey-bodied Leylands constituted the largest batch of consecutively registered buses ever supplied to a Tees-side municipal operator. Here too, several of them were substantially rebuilt by the Corporation, commencing in 1959, and the work considerably altered the external appearance. This is shown on No. **64** (**KPT 769**), photographed in the High Street in 1961. *(Geoffrey Holt)*

Above: Stockton took a further substantial batch of Leylands in 1950, this time with Weymann's bodies. The destinations were displayed with greater clarity than before, as can be seen on No. **24 (LPT 202)** as it passes the parish church in the late 1950s. *(R H G Simpson)*

Below: Middlesbrough's need for single-deck trams, and then for lowbridge buses, is graphically demonstrated by this view of the Albert Bridge underneath the railway station. The Guy Arab is No. **29 (BXG 129)** of 1951. It marked the beginning of a period of forty-four years in which every new double-decker bought by Middlesbrough Corporation and its successors was bodied at the Northern Counties factory at Wigan. *(John Fozard Collection)*

Above: An example of the highbridge Guy, also on a tram replacement service, was No. **1** (**CDC 401**) of 1952. It demonstrates the route letter O used jointly with Stockton, who of course regarded it as a number. This stop at Middlesbrough Town Hall used to have huge queues at peak hours, a situation eased by roving conductors and as many duplicates as could be mustered. *(Geoffrey Holt)*

Below: Another of the batch was No. **6** (**CDC 406**), photographed under the trolleybus wires at North Ormesby. The TRTB motor buses on the left were Nos **39** and **21** (**FAJ 185** and **PVN 21**) which were operating the trolleybus service one weekend in 1966 during extensive alterations to the overhead.

Above: Nineteen-fifty-four was the last year of production of bus bodies at Leyland, when seven PD2/12s were turned out for Stockton. Here is No. **7 (OUP 756)** in 1967 at the quaintly named Paddy's Crossing in the middle of the ICI works at Billingham. It is operating one of the many works services, in this case suitably labelled "Stockton via Paddy's Crossing".

Below: In sharply contrasting circumstances, No. **4 (OUP 753)** was turning at Billingham's northern extremity in 1968 on an infrequent new service. There are of course no passengers - the houses were hardly built at this stage - but the development of a school campus gave rise to the destination "Campus School", a peculiar inversion created by people who probably did not know what a campus is.

Above: Middlesbrough's 1954 Guy Arabs were renowned for a specification which reverted to the exposed radiator. A less well known peculiarity was the experimental advertising screen fitted in the lower saloon of No. **36** (**DXG 136**) in 1956. It was simply a powered roller blind, but a marvel of the age which fascinated schoolboys. This official photograph shows dragooned office staff studiously ignoring the contraption. *(Author's Collection)*

Below: The Leyland Olympic was never common, and the two-door version purchased by Stockton in 1951 was a particular attraction for enthusiasts. It was mainly used on the infrequent rural service 8A, but gained a new lease of life in 1964 after being rebuilt for one-man operation with only a single door. In this form No. **26** (**MPT 858**) was photographed at Chilton Lane in 1966 on service 1 (Stockton - Transporter), looking lost in ICI's East Gate bus station which was intensively served at shift times.

Above: The 1955 Guy Arabs at Middlesbrough were in their turn long-lived stalwarts of the busy O service, and here No. **92** (**EXG 892**) passes the former Smith's Safeway Services garage in North Ormesby Road. The board in the upper saloon front window announced the supplementary fares charged at weekends, and dates the picture to 1963. *(Author's collection)*

Below: Temporary diversions provided some awkward manoeuvres for drivers and added interest for enthusiasts. In Cambridge Road, Middlesbrough, in 1967 Guy Arab, No. **90** (**EXG 890**), turns into Thornfield Grove whilst the car driver is oblivious to the trouble she is causing. The driver of similar bus No. **35** (**DXG 135**) on the 11 service pauses to let his colleague through.

Above: Stockton was also buying Northern Counties bodies in 1955, but on Leyland PD2/12 chassis. They seemed much plainer than the Middlesbrough ones, but ran in tandem with them on the 0 service. In later years, No. **30** (**RUP 304**) had been relegated to a special duty when photographed in January 1968.

Below: From 1951, all new Guys for Middlesbrough had the patented "Induction Ventilation System" in which the engine drew its air from the smoky atmosphere of the upper saloon. Great claims were made for how many times an hour the upper saloon air was changed - but how often did mechanics fail to reconnect the pipes after servicing the engine? The device accounted for the wide pillar at the front of the upper deck, seen here on lowbridge No. **15** (**GDC 315**) of 1957 in Roman Road in 1965.

Above: After 1950 the TRTB made no additions to the fleet until 1957, but then did so with style. This is the second of two smart Leyland Tiger Cubs with Roe Dalesman coach bodies. By the time of this 1961 view of No. **51** (**PVN 51**), the linesman's tower had been transferred to the chassis of 1939 Leyland Tiger No. **25** (**BAJ 846**), and the resulting vehicle can be seen in the background. *(Geoffrey Holt)*

Below: The 1957 deliveries at Stockton comprised Leyland PD2/12 chassis with Crossley and Northern Counties bodies. Of the latter, No. **94** (**VUP 459**) was photographed in the High Street in the 1960s. This was a period when new PD2s were replacing old ones, and that model accounted for all but one member of the fleet. It was also a period when the destination displays were used less effectively, as is the case here. *(R A Stone)*

47

Above: Middlesbrough received further lowbridge Guys in 1958, and No. **22** (**JDC 222**) was waiting to depart from the Exchange on a "Special K" working in the 1960s. At that time the destination display carried no overtones about a breakfast cereal. *(R A Stone)*

Below: Middlesbrough's buses had not terminated at Port Clarence since the leaving of the Seaton Carew service entirely in the hands of West Hartlepool Corporation in 1927. Exceptions could occur when the Newport Bridge over the River Tees was closed for repairs, and Guy Arab No. **23** (**JDC 223**) was photographed on one such occasion in 1966. The joint 11 service from Billingham brought passengers to the Transporter bridge, by which means they then reached Middlesbrough. The Stockton bus behind is on the regular service 2.

Above: In the days when schoolboys could still look neat and tidy, some of the breed were photographed boarding Stockton's No. **39 (XUP 478)** in Cambridge Road, Middlesbrough, in 1967. The 1958 Leyland carried Northern Counties bodywork, and had the distinctive rear directional trafficators on which Stockton had standardised at an early date.

Below: The bus in the background in the above picture, Middlesbrough's now-preserved 67-seat Dennis Loline No. **99 (JDC 599)**, was a star of the 1958 Commercial Motor Show; in this picture it is seen in its first week of service at The Crescent, Middlesbrough. A low-height bus with conventional upper-deck layout, it heralded a new era in which there was no place for the traditional sunken-gangway style of lowbridge double decker. Note that the induction ventilation has been superseded by the Cave-Browne-Cave system.

Above: From 1957 the Tees-side Railless had been rebuilding the wartime utility trolleybus bodies, with some of the work undertaken by Edmond's. As at Stockton, this work considerably altered the external appearance, shown here on Roe-bodied No. **10** (**CPY 308**). It was at North Ormesby on driver training duties in 1961. *(Geoffrey Holt)*

Below: From 1960 the Board gradually dismantled all its trolleybus bodies, beginning with an accident victim. The chassis then went to Roe's to be rebodied. In this 1961 scene, the Weymann's body on No. **17** (**CPY 288**) had been partly stripped, and behind can be seen two ex-Mexborough and Swinton Sunbeam chassis which had been acquired for spares. *(Geoffrey Holt)*

Above: Later in 1958 Stockton turned to Weymann's again, and a rather solid version of the Orion body graced all deliveries to the undertaking for the next five years. The 1958 batch were the last to have the three cream bands in the livery, which looked fine at the time, as can be seen here on No. **82** (**208 BPT**). It later came to look a bit cluttered when our eyes had become used to a more spartan presentation. *(Geoffrey Holt)*

Below: Stockton was the first of the three operators to apply a turquoise livery in anticipation of the amalgamation, which took place in 1968. This is demonstrated by Park Royal-bodied No. **71** (**XUP 471**), operating a works special to the Furness Shipyard in 1967. The long-gone "Empire" buildings and a 1964 Leyland Atlantean can be seen in the background in this High Street view.

Above: After the startling impact of Middlesbrough's Loline No. 99, an order for eight arrived as front-entrance vehicles in 1960. The rear view, shown on No. **41 (LXG 241)** opposite the Town Hall in 1963, illustrates the full destination display fitted at the back.

Below: Despite the urgency felt about having more suitable low height vehicles for the M service, Middlesbrough soon moved the Lolines with their 70 seats on to routes serving the heavily populated housing estates to the south-east of the town. In a busy mid 1960s scene at North Ormesby Market Place, No. **47 (LXG 247)** was pictured working to the Brambles Farm estate, a name displayed with characteristic brevity. *(R A Stone)*

Above: At the end of 1960 the TRTB received the first two of its rebodied trolleybuses, which seated 61. A few months later, No. **18** (**CPY 289**) was photographed approaching the depot from North Ormesby. Wimpey the contractor had the AEC Regal which was **KKK 825** from Maidstone & District. *(Geoffrey Holt)*

Below: The Roe-bodied Leyland PD2 was to be the standard new bus for the TRTB from 1957 to 1967, and No. **23** (**SVN 23**) of 1958 is seen here passing Warner's Foundry at Cargo Fleet. In 1966 the poster advertised the first Tees-side International Industrial Eisteddfod, held at nearby Wilton I.C.I. under the chairmanship of Dr S Jenkin Evans, and was a notable exception to the no-advertising policy. The other bus belonged to the ever-present United Automobile Services Ltd.

Above: The same 1958 bus is seen again at the centre island at Eston Square, which accommodated bus stops for more than forty years. The arrangement required the buses to negotiate the island anti-clockwise. In this 1968 picture, the poles do not reveal a former trolleybus service, but one which was shortly to be introduced. This was to create a circular route by linking the Normanby and Grangetown termini. One consequence was that traffic then moved clockwise round the Square, and the bus stops were moved off the island.

Below: This classic view of the T service at work shows the reason for its separate existence. The Leyland PD2/27 of 1961, No. **28 (YAJ 28)**, is in the very act of passing the trolleybus turning circle at North Ormesby on its way into central Middlesbrough. A sensor, visible on the traction pole, kept the lights at red when the circle was in use. The trolleybuses had "Middlesbrough" printed hopefully on the destination blinds, but the hopes were never realised. *(R F Mack)*

54

Above: Stockton's last open platform buses were delivered in 1961, completing a small group of four more 63-seat Leyland PD2/40s. This picture dates from the same year, with No. **43 (762 HPT)** operating to the new and still growing Hardwick estate which nowadays boasts Tees-side's most frequent service. *(Geoffrey Holt)*

Below: Middlesbrough Corporation and United had each introduced the forward entrance double decker in 1960. Stockton followed with seven in 1962, of the established Leyland PD2/Weymann's combination. In a 1966 photograph, an inspector uses the internal telephone system whilst No. **102 (8632 PT)** waits to leave for Yarm on the route which saw Stockton's first bus service in 1914. The unbalanced front window arrangement was the result of an accident. *(John Heighway)*

Above: The Stockton forward entrance PD2s had hardly entered service when Middlesbrough went one better with the first rear-engined buses in the district. These were ten Daimler Fleetlines, dramatically displaying "Air Brakes" warning triangles on the back. In this exposed wintry scene on Cargo Fleet Lane, Thorntree, in 1965 No. **113** (**PDC 113**) works the "Link" service, which although horseshoe in shape would have been called Outer Circle anywhere else.

Below: Later in 1962 Stockton borrowed a Daimler Fleetline demonstrator, the much travelled **7000 HP**. It was pictured working service 6 in Thornaby at Christmas, 1962, showing the Congregational church and the Harewood Arms in a scene that has nowadays entirely disappeared.

Above: The tram replacement service of 1932 extended to the busy Market Place at North Ormesby, where Stockton's Weymann-bodied No. **27** (**RUP 301**) stands at the terminus in 1965 whilst Middlesbrough's 1963 Fleetline No. **121** (**RDC 121**) loads on the very busy Y service. In timetables and notices Middlesbrough described this location as NOMP, which must have puzzled strangers to the town. Some other services terminated at the Tees Valley Water Board offices in the town centre, described as TVWB with similar effect.

Below: Buses of all three Tees-side municipal operators can be seen in this 1965 view of the Exchange bus station in Middlesbrough. The TRTB Roe-bodied Leyland Leopard No. **33** (**CAJ 433C**) had been new earlier in the year. In the background, among three Middlesbrough Fleetlines, can be seen Stockton's Crossley-bodied No. **99** (**VUP 464**) on the Stockton via Acklam 11 service.

Above: In 1964 Stockton decided to change to the rear-engined bus and stayed with Leyland, but the body contract went to Park Royal. As the first of a new design, this became known as the Stockton body, achieving more renown when a much larger batch was supplied to London Transport. The box-on-wheels effect, shown here on No. **A4 (BPT 514B)** when new, was intensified by the pronounced rattling felt and heard by passengers. *(Geoffrey Holt)*

Below: An even more dramatic new design came to Middlesbrough in 1966 with two Leyland Panther Cubs bodied by Northern Counties. These took over the Seamer and Link services for which they had been purchased, and No. **1 (DXG 401D)** was pictured at the Exchange when newly in service.

Above: Although United and its predecessors operated from Middlesbrough to West Hartlepool, the shortest and quickest way was often to use the Transporter bridge to Port Clarence and then travel by West Hartlepool Corporation. In a quiet moment in 1966, No. **18 (MEF 618)** was unloading at its Transporter terminus. The Roe-bodied Leyland PD2/40 of 1962 had an obvious affinity to the TRTB vehicles of the period. *(Author's Collection)*

Below: Another Tees-side destination regularly served by West Hartlepool Corporation was the Furness Shipyard. WHCT had recently been merged into the new Hartlepool undertaking at the time of this busy home-time scene in 1967, when United, Middlesbrough, Stockton and independent buses jostled with each other but were beaten by a Hillman Minx and a brave cyclist. Whilst Hartlepool's No. **27 (BEF 27C)** would remain in dark red and cream, the Stockton Atlantean, No. **A12 (EPT 912B)**, had already received its turquoise livery.

Left: A severe instance of trolley trouble was the exception rather than the rule, but this one occurred near Grangetown in 1966. All the trolleybuses were carrying new Roe bodies by this date, and whilst No. **7** (**GAJ 17**) has come to grief, No. **2** (**GAJ 12**) passes by dint of wrong-way working. The Bedford tower lorry FET196 had come from Rotherham a few months earlier. *(John Banks)*

Below: As the 1968 amalgamation date approached, the turquoise livery became widespread. In Middlesbrough's case this was assisted by a very lengthy strike which gave the painters uninhibited access to the fleet. Repainted lowbridge Guy No. **23** (**JDC 223**) already looks a bit shabby as it approaches Thornaby Baths, with passengers hopping off in the time honoured tradition which now is no more.

Above: Final deliveries to the established operators were in the turquoise livery. They included ten Fleetlines for Middlesbrough with a new style of front incorporating wrap-round windscreens. When No. **73** (**FXG 873E**) was new in 1967, with its full complement of coats-of-arms, it was seen passing Hinton's Café and Grocer's, another local tradition now long gone.

Below: Nineteen-sixty-seven was also the date when the motor registration year was changed to commence in August, so when Stockton received ten Leyland Panthers later that year, they had "F" registrations. In due course these buses were used for one-man operation, for which they were designed, but in the meantime No. **S8** (**VUP 908F**) was on service 2 at Haverton Hill when photographed early in 1968.

Above: The opening of the Eston trolleybus extension on the very last day of the Tees-side Railless Traction Board's existence, 31st March 1968, is well known. What is often overlooked is the arrival of six Roe-bodied Leyland Atlanteans shortly beforehand. By the time of this 1970 photograph, **MVN 47F** had the Teesside Municipal Transport fleetname and had been renumbered from 47 to **A25**, but the destination blind with yellow route letter is still pure TRTB. The scene is Smeaton Street, North Ormesby.

Below: The addition of service number blinds was an awkward task for the new TMT undertaking, and the results were often ungainly. This example is better than some, and is seen in 1974 on No. **S304** (**CAJ 434C**) ex-TRTB 34, on the hourly Hemlington - Stockton service which owed more to idealism than to practicality.

Above: Teesside Municipal Transport made several unusual secondhand purchases to tide it over a difficult period. To augment the extended trolleybus system, five forward-entrance 1962 Sunbeam F4s, bodied by Burlingham, came from Reading in 1969. They took the numbers 8-12 within the existing trolleybus sequence, and Nos **9** and **12** (**VRD 184/92**) were newly in service when photographed passing the depot on a very wet day.

Below: The final alteration to the trolleybus system was caused by roadworks at North Ormesby, where the turning circle was removed in 1970. Reversal was then achieved by use of a spur erected in Hampden Street, seen here being used by No. **16** (**CPY 287**) that same year.

Above: The attractive Georgian High Street and Town Hall at Yarm are the setting for this 1971 view of ex-Stockton 106, by this time numbered **H206** (**8636 PT**).

Below: The 1971 trolleybus replacement vehicles of Teesside Municipal Transport heralded a new era with a new standard that was recognisably Teesside. Outside Middlesbrough Town Hall in 1972 is TMT fleet number **L502** (**VXG 502J**), a low-height two-door Daimler Fleetline of a type that was eventually to total 76. At the end of the book, and with the dawn of this new era, it is time to say goodbye to what we have known and loved.